The Prayer Toolbox

50+ Ideas to Inspire
Your Prayer Life

Kathryn Shirey

Published by San Marco Publications Frisco, TX

ISBN: 978-1-7344819-6-9

The Prayer Toolbox

Do you want to reinvigorate your prayer life, making it a more vibrant part of your life? Do you want to hear God's voice more clearly in your life? Do you struggle with prayer and wish you could find a way to make it more meaningful and impactful for your life?

The Prayer Toolbox provides more than 50 prayer ideas to refresh, renew, and inspire your prayer life so you can grow ever closer to God.

What is the Prayer Toolbox?

Prayer is not 'one size fits all' or a prescriptive template. The Prayer Toolbox is a collection of prayer methods and ideas to grow your prayer life. Explore different aspects of your relationship with God and find different ways to enhance your conversations with Him through prayer.

Why Use Different Prayer Methods?

God created us to be unique individuals with different learning and communication styles and a variety of gifts and talents. He desires to connect with us in the ways in which he wired us. Some of us love silence, while others bristle at the thought of sitting still. Some of us communicate through art and music, while others communicate best through words.

Variety also helps keep prayer vibrant. If you feel yourself slipping into a prayer rut or falling out of your prayer discipline, change it up by trying a new form of prayer. Choose something different (even uncomfortable) and let it reinvigorate your prayer time. You may even find a new favorite!

How Do I Use This Prayer Toolbox?

The booklet is divided into five sections - Prayer Basics, Praying Through Scripture, Listening Prayer, Prayer Through Art & Music, and Prayer Through Movement. Within these, you'll find 16 different prayer methods, plus several ideas to incorporate each method in your own prayer time. Use this Prayer Toolbox to guide your prayers and inspire your prayer life.

"And pray in the Spirit on all occasions with all kinds of prayers and requests. With this in mind, be alert and always keep on praying for all the Lord's people."
~Ephesians 6:18 (NIV)

Explore Ways to Pray

I encourage you to try as many forms of prayer as you can. See which ones fit for you. God made us each unique and speaks to us each in our own ways. So, your prayers don't have to look like someone else's. Pray in the ways that fit you best.

"There are as many temperaments as there are men, and each has his own problems and his peculiar way of expressing the Spirit of Christ."
~Harry Emerson Fosdick

Discover Forms of Prayer That Fit You

Use the table below to find prayer formats that sound interesting or fit best with how God made you. Many of these prayers are included in The Prayer Toolbox.

You can find details on praying all of these forms of prayer on the Prayer & Possibilities website (www.PrayerandPossibilities.com).

Or, join our Pray Deep course for an in-depth study on all aspects of prayer, including guides on 22 different ways to pray. Learn more at: https://www.prayerandpossibilities.com/pray-deep-prayer-course

	• Do you prefer structure and order to your prayers? • Do you struggle with what to say or how to say it? • Do you need some help getting started in your prayer time?	You may like using PRAYER TEMPLATES or PREWRITTEN PRAYERS: • The Lord's Prayer • ACTS prayer method • 5 Finger Prayer • The Book of Common Prayer or other books of prayers • Prayer Prompts

	• Do you like to pray through Scripture, praying God's Word back to him? • Do you want to expand your prayer language, learning to incorporate scripture into your prayers? • Do you want to hear from God in powerful ways?	You may like **PRAYING THROUGH SCRIPTURE**: • Praying through Scripture • Praying Psalms • Lectio Divina • Gospel Contemplation
	• Do you express yourself better through writing? • Do you enjoy journaling?	You may like **WRITING YOUR PRAYERS**: • Prayer Journaling • Writing Prayers for Others
	• Do you like to sing or express yourself through music? • Do you connect to song lyrics as an expression of your own emotions?	You may like **PRAYING THROUGH MUSIC**: • Singing a Prayer • Praying Through Hymn Lyrics • Taize Prayer

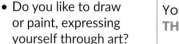	• Do you like to draw or paint, expressing yourself through art? • Do you find that doodling or drawing helps your mind focus? • Do you connect through visuals, such as paintings, photos, or scenes in nature?	You may like **PRAYING THROUGH ART**: • Prayer Doodles • Prayer Collage • Visio Divina • Praying Mandalas
	• Do you find that movement helps you focus and express your thoughts? • Do you enjoy quiet, reflective walks?	You may like **PRAYING THROUGH MOVEMENT**: • Prayer Walking • Labyrinth
	• Do you want to hear God more clearly in your life? • Do you like silence and listening? • Do you need to spend time in reflection and examination with God?	You may like **LISTENING PRAYERS**: • Listening Prayer • Centering Prayer • Examen
	• Do you like praying with other people? • Do you like to hear other peoples' voices as they pray for you?	You may like **PRAYING WITH OTHERS**: • Praying with a Prayer Partner • Corporate Prayer • Praying Out Loud

Prayer Basics

Whether you're just getting started in your prayer life or a seasoned prayer warrior looking to reinvigorate your prayer life, the basics are a great place to start.

What Is Prayer?

Prayer is our conversation with God. He invites us into prayer to share our lives with Him. Just as you'd cover a variety of topics in conversations with your best friend, so God wants us to open a variety of dialogs with Him.

Key Components of Prayer:

1) **Start with praise.** Begin your conversation with a compliment or gracious greeting. Open your prayer with words of praise.

2) **Say thank you.** Express your gratitude for who God is and what He's done. This not only shows your appreciation to God, but it also sets your heart and mind in the right place for prayer.

3) **Share what's going on in your life.** Bring God into the conversations and decisions in your life. Share your concerns, your struggles, and where you need His help.

4) **Apologize.** God is ready to forgive and abundantly pour out his grace and mercy, but you have to come before Him and confess your sins.

5) **Make requests for yourself and others.** Prayers of petition and intercession are a critical component of prayer. Pray specifically and boldly for your needs and those of others. You may not see the prayer answered or see it answered the way you expected, but keep praying.

6) **Listen.** Prayer is a two-way conversation, so allow God space to enter the conversation. Don't fill all the space with your words. You may not always hear Him, but develop a practice of listening and give him the opportunity to speak to your heart.

"One day Jesus was praying in a certain place. When he finished, one of his disciples said to him, "Lord, teach us to pray, just as John taught his disciples."
~Luke 11:1 (NIV)

The Lord's Prayer

Our Father, who art in heaven,
    hallowed be thy Name,
    thy kingdom come,
    thy will be done,
        on earth as it is in heaven.
Give us this day our daily bread.
And forgive us our trespasses,
    as we forgive those who trespass against us.
And lead us not into temptation,
    but deliver us from evil.
For thine is the kingdom, and the power, and the glory,
    for ever and ever. Amen.

Prayer Ideas...

Below are three ways to pray the Lord's Prayer and rediscover its power in your life:

1) Pray the Lord's Prayer by reading it slowly, considering each line and what it means in your life today.

2) Pray one line of the Lord's Prayer each day, focusing on just that single line. Journal your prayers or write down your observations of what you hear from God through each line.

3) Write your own version of the Lord's Prayer, putting each line into your own words. Include specifics of how each line applies to your life today.

"I used to think the Lord's Prayer was short prayer; but as I live longer, and see more of life, I begin to believe there is no such thing as getting through it. If a man, in praying that prayer, were to be stopped by every word until he had thoroughly prayed it, it would take him a lifetime." ~Henry Ward Beecher

Prayer Ideas...

The A.C.T.S. template for prayer provides an easy acronym to remember the essentials of the Lord's Prayer.

1) Use this acronym to pray through these four areas during your prayer time.

2) Focus on one letter at a time. Which one have you been neglecting in your prayer life? Take that letter and pray just that one for the day (or week).

3) If you aren't able to cover all four areas in one prayer session or want to have more time for each, split them over the course of the day. Begin your day with Adoration. Over lunch, pray Confession. At dinner, pray Thanksgiving. Before you go to bed, pray Supplication.

A.C.T.S Prayer Template

A **DORATION**
Tell God how wonderful He is. Worship Him and acknowledge His goodness.

C **ONFESSION**
Admit your sins. Cry out your brokenness. Ask for God's forgiveness, grace, and mercy.

T **HANKSGIVING**
Say "thank you" to God for all He's done in your life.

S **UPPLICATION**
Make your requests to God, asking Him for your own needs and for those of others.

Prayer Ideas...

The 5 Finger Prayer is attributed to Pope Francis, developed long before he became the Pope. It is a guide for prayers of petition and intercession. It's also a great tool for teaching children to pray.

1) Use this prayer as a template to help you pray through your prayer list.

2) Each week, determine who you'll pray for as each finger. This could be one particular person per finger or several. Throughout your day, make a habit of praying through your fingers.

3) Use this prayer with your children or grandchildren. Teach them the prayers for each finger and pray with them.

4) Pray for the sick and needy

5) Pray for yourself

3) Pray for leaders and government

2) Pray for teachers and helpers

1) Pray for family and friends

5 Finger Prayer

Prayer Prompts

Every day prayer prompts are a way to weave prayer throughout your day. These are reminders to pray and can help develop your prayer habits and create a daily dialog with God.

- Choose something or someone you see frequently throughout your week. Some suggestions:
  - Something you love (your child, nature)
  - Something that frustrates you (red lights, a co-worker)
  - Someone who needs prayer (firemen, the homeless)
- Decide on a brief prayer you'll say each time you see that prompt.
- When you see that prompt, say your brief prayer.
- Say your prayer quietly or make it a family activity and say it together.

Prayer Ideas...

Make a list of possible prayer prompts and what each would remind you to pray. Choose one to add into your day. As you begin to incorporate that one prayer prompt into your daily routine, add in another. Consider having 2-3 prayer prompts.

Some ideas...

- Firetruck or ambulance: *Pray for first responders and those who risk their lives to keep us safe.*
- Stopped at a red light: *Pause and thank God for a blessing in your life.*
- See the homeless person on the corner: *Pray for all those in need, particularly the homeless and most destitute.*
- See the sunrise or sunset: *Praise God for His majesty and glory in all His creation.*
- Hug your child: *Pray for God's protection and blessings over your child.*
- See someone who frustrates you: *Pray for God's blessings on that person and your heart to be softened toward them.*

Praying Through Scripture

Praying through scripture is one of the most powerful ways to engage with God and expand your own prayer language. It's a way to pray His words and promises back to Him, while also allowing those scripture verses to sink deep into your heart.

Expand Your Prayer Language

Ever listened to others praying and thought 'I wish I could find those kind of words to pray'? Or heard the prayers from the Prayer Book at church and wanted to pray with similar power and poetry? Praying through scripture will expand your prayer language, giving you a new vocabulary of God's words. You'll learn new ways to praise and adore God, new ways to pray through His promises and call upon His power, and new ways to ask for God's mercy, forgiveness, and grace.

Hear God's Response Through His Words

Do you desire to hear God's voice more clearly in your life? Tired of hearing others talk about hearing from God, but you haven't yet heard Him answer your prayers? While there's no guarantee you'll hear from God directly or hear from Him in the same way as someone else, one of the best ways to open your heart to Him is through scripture. The Bible is the living Word of God and He uses its words to speak into your heart. Spending more time in the Word, and particularly using scripture in prayers, is a great way to open your heart to hear God's response.

Use Jesus' Own Prayer Book

Jesus often quoted from the Psalms and even prayed from Psalm 22:1 at the end when he cried out, "My God, my God why have you forsaken me?" The Psalms have been used as the church's prayer book for centuries as they cover every human emotion and need. You can find Psalms to praise and adore God, ask for guidance, ask for forgiveness and mercy, cry out for help, or express your deepest despair.

"The Psalter is the prayer book of Jesus Christ... He prayed the Psalter and now it has become his prayer book for all time... Those who pray the psalms are joining in with the prayer of Jesus Christ, their prayer reaches the ears of God. Christ has become their intercessor. "
~ Dietrich Bonhoeffer in Life Together

Prayer Ideas...

Select a scripture to pray and then use the steps listed below to dig into God's Word and pray it back to Him.

1) Take the readings from your church service and pray through each of them during the week. Or, use the readings from the Common Lectionary (www.lectionarypage.net).

2) Keep a list of favorite verses or specific promises and hopes for different needs. Choose one of these verses to pray. Listen for fresh insights as you read and pray.

3) Open your Bible and place your finger on the page. Pray that scripture.

4) As you read the scripture, write it in your journal or on a notecard. Use different colors, illustrate the words, or doodle around it as you spend time absorbing the words. Keep the card with you through the day to call your mind back to the prayer you prayed.

Praying Scripture

Choose a scripture passage to pray. Passages from the Gospel or Epistles are a great place to start, but you can use any scripture for your prayer.

READ the passage a few times to absorb the words.

REFLECT on what the passage means to you. What does it say about God? What does it say about our human nature? What does it say about you?

RESPOND to God, praying the passage back to Him.
> **REJOICE** in God's great goodness.
> **REPENT** your sins and shortcomings.
> **REQUEST** God's help.

RECEIVE God's response to you by listening.

Prayer Ideas...

Chose a Psalm to pray and follow the below steps to pray through the Psalm.

1) Use the Psalm read during your church service and pray through it during the week. If one wasn't read or you aren't sure which one, use the selected Psalm from the Common Lectionary (www. lectionarypage.net).

2) Start at the beginning of Psalms and pray your way through the book, praying one Psalm each day or each week.

3) Find a Psalm that meets your prayer needs. Make your own list of Psalms for different needs or find listings of Psalms online. One resource is The Psalm Finder (www.kencollins.com/psalmfinder.htm).

4) Pray a Psalm in its nature setting. Go to http://www. soulshepherding.org/2009/08/pray-a-psalm-in-its-nature-setting/ for a list of ideas.

Praying Psalms

Choose a Psalm and read through it. Linger over the words.

Are there particular verses that stand out to you today? Are there any specific words that speak to your heart?

Read those verses aloud over and over, emphasizing each word.

Write out those verses in your own words, with the emphasis you hear as you read them aloud.

Pray for yourself and others from those verses.

Commit these words to your heart and begin to incorporate them into your prayers.

Lectio Divina

Choose a brief scripture passage to read.

READ the verse slowly, several times, listening with the "ear of your heart". You can also use an audio Bible to listen as the passage is read.

REFLECT on the words, attentive to which word or phrase speaks most to your heart. *What is God's message to you in your life or the life of others?*

RESPOND to the words that spoke to you, turning them over and over in your heart. Offer it up in prayer. *What is your prayer for yourself in light of God's message?*

REST in God. Sit in silence and listen for how God is speaking to you through that word or phrase. *What is your experience of God now and how does this help?*

Prayer Ideas...

Lectio Divina translated as "Divine Reading," a way to listen with the "ear of your heart" for God's still small voice through the reading of scripture.

1) Choose a passage of scripture and use the steps above to pray through Lectio Divina.

2) Use a guided Lectio Divina reading. alivenow.upperroom.org provides guided Lectio Divina using the week's scripture from the Lectionary. These are audio-based. soulshepherding.org provides printed Lectio Divina guides for a variety of scriptures.

3) Use Lectio Divina as a group. Guide your small group through prayer using Lectio Divina.

Find additional listings of online resources at:
htpps://attentivenesstogod.wordpress.com/daily-examen/

Gospel Contemplation

Select a scripture where Jesus is interacting with others.

Read the passage a few times until the story is familiar.

Close your eyes. Play the scene in your mind like a movie. Fully experience the scene in your imagination using all your senses.

What do you see? What sounds do you hear? What do you smell? What is Jesus saying? What is the reaction and attitude of the people around you? What emotion and demeanor do you see in Jesus? How is he interacting with others? How do you experience the scene? What emotion does it stir in your heart?

Pray and speak your heart to Jesus from this experience.

Prayer Ideas...

Praying through Gospel Contemplation is a way to make Jesus even more real and personal in your life - not just the Jesus in scripture, but YOUR Jesus.

1) Use the week's Gospel reading and pray through the steps above to more deeply and personally experience the passage.

2) Choose one of the Gospels and pray through it, story by story. Embed yourself into the narrative and experience firsthand the life of Jesus.

3) During particular seasons of the year, pray through related passages.

- During Advent, pray through the birth and early years of Christ passages from all four Gospels.

- During Lent, pray through Jesus' ministry and the calling of the disciples.

- During Holy Week, pray through Jesus' final week and crucifixion.

- During Pentecost, pray through Jesus' resurrection and the coming of the Holy Spirit.

Listening Prayer

If prayer is a conversation with God, why does it so often feel one-sided, even lonely? Learning to hear God's voice in your prayers takes focus and practice. You need to learn the Father's voice and how He speaks into your heart. Then you need to regularly give Him the silence and space to speak.

Give God the Space to Speak

Are your prayers typically more full of words than silence? Do you fill your prayers with words and then quickly close with an 'amen' and move on? If you did that in conversations with other friends, they'd be left standing there saying, "but, I wanted to say something, too..."

It may feel awkward to add silence and listening into your prayers. Maybe you haven't heard God's response before and or aren't sure He'll actually respond to your prayers. Give Him an opportunity by adding some quiet time and listening into your prayers.

Learn God's Voice In Your Life

Just as a mother can pick out her child's voice above all the others on a loud playground, so you can learn to hear God's voice in your life. He will speak to you in different ways, in just the way He created you to hear Him. Cultivating a rich prayer life, including time to listen, will help you find His voice in your life.

Practice Silence and Listening

Listening prayer takes practice. You may not hear God right away, so don't get discouraged. Press on and build a practice in your life to listen for God. Start small - just a few minutes - and work your way up to more. Begin with scripture and listen for God's voice through His Word. When you do hear something, validate it against scripture, confirmations from other Christians, and God's work in your life. If you've heard something from God, you can expect Him to confirm it in numerous ways.

"My sheep listen to my voice; I know them, and they follow me. I give them eternal life, and they shall never perish; no one will snatch them out of my hand."
~John 10:27-28 (NIV)

Prayer Ideas...

Tips for praying a Listening Prayer:

- If it's hard to clear your mind and million thoughts are flying by, write each one down for later, then let them go. Do this until your mind is clear for prayer.

- Start with a breathing exercise. One is to count down from 50. On each inhale and exhale, count down by ones from 50. Continue to count backward until you get to 20. Then only count on the exhales. Count down to 0 and then enter into prayer.

- Start small and work your into longer prayers over time. Set a timer so you're not tempted to look at the clock.

- Use one color for God's words to you and another color for your thoughts as you journal and respond to God.

"God speaks in the silence of the heart. Listening is the beginning of prayer"
~Mother Teresa

Listening Prayer

Set aside some quiet time when you can focus.

Start by relaxing your body. Take some deep breaths or do a breathing exercise to calm and clear your mind.

Close your eyes and settle into the silence.

Ask God to enter the silence and speak into your heart.

Sit in the silence and listen for God. Start with 3 minutes. Work your way up to 15 minutes or more over time.

Take notes or journal what God places on your heart. What is your response to God? What action will you take?

Close with prayers of thanksgiving and praise, offering up your response and asking God's help to step into it.

Examen

Set aside some quiet time for reflection. Maybe at the end of each day or even a mid-day review.

Ask for God's presence in your prayers. Ask the Holy Spirit for guidance as you pray. Thank God for the day's blessings.

Walk through the day, reviewing your actions and interactions. Imagine you are talking with Jesus.

- Ask him to show you two areas that were great and two where you could improve.
- Talk to him about your reactions and emotions in the day.

Close with prayer to reconcile and resolve.

- Give thanks for where you did well.
- Apologize for where you fell short.
- Ask for guidance and support to do better tomorrow.

Prayer Ideas...

Praying the Examen is a way to have a 'daily debrief' with Jesus on your day (or week) to celebrate the victories, learn from your mistakes, and do better next time.

Below are some ways to incorporate Examen into your prayer life:

1) Pray the Examen at the end of each day or week. Schedule this time with God. Keep a journal of what you hear and how you respond, so you can see your progress over time.

2) Use an online guide to help you pray the Examen. Examen.me and www.ignatianspirituality.com/ignatian-prayer/the-examen provide a number of resources.

"We must lay before him what is in us; not what ought to be in us."
~C.S. Lewis

Prayer Through Art & Music

While praying through your own words, through scripture, and through listening are essential, God also created you as a creative being. He gave you art and music and wired you to communicate through them.

I'm Not Artistic. Is This For Me?

You don't need to be artistic or creative to pray though art and music. It's not about the end product, but about the process of prayer.

Using art and music in your prayers can help keep your prayer time engaging and fresh, help quiet your inner monologue, and help you break out of a prayer rut and reignite your prayer life if your prayers have begin to feel stale.

Active Prayer To Quiet The Mind

Coloring and doing art can be a way to bring more quiet and focus to your prayers. As your hands are busy coloring, your mind becomes free to listen for God. Doing something active, yet not thought-provoking, can bring greater focus to your mind and help you stay more engaged in your prayers.

Prayer Through Creating

You can pray through creating art and music. Just as God created you with a unique learning and communication style, so can you communicate in your own way with God. You can pray through coloring, drawing, or painting. You can pray through singing or creating music. Each is a way to offer yourself to God and create a space to listen for His voice.

Prayer Through Experiencing

You can also pray through experiencing art and music. Incorporate music into your prayer time, either listening or singing. Use art as a tool to enhance your worship and prayer time, using paintings, icons, or even stained glass windows to bring a focus to your prayers.

"Grant that I may not pray alone with the mouth;
help me that I may pray from the depths of my heart."
~ Martin Luther

Prayer Doodles

On a blank sheet of paper, write a name for God, the name of someone you're praying for, or a scripture verse.

Draw a shape around it and begin to fill in around it with doodles and embellishments.

As you draw, pray and lift this prayer request up to God. Ask God to be part of this prayer time.

Continue praying by adding additional names, needs, or scriptures, lifting each in prayer as you draw. You may want to say an 'amen' between each to close out each specific prayer.

Find more information at www.prayingincolor.com

Prayer Ideas...

Prayer doodles are a way to incorporate art and movement into your prayer time to help bring more focus and quiet to your prayers. It's a great way to pray for others, particularly when you aren't sure what words to use.

Below are a few ways to pray through prayer doodles:

1) Pray God's promises. Pray through the names and promises of God, writing these on your sheet and drawing around them as you pray.

2) Pray over your prayer request list. Write each name and then spend time lifting that person or need to God in prayer as you draw around it. Continue to do the same for each other name and need on your list.

3) Pray (and memorize) a scripture verse. Write each word or phrase of a verse. Doodle around each as you pray and commit it to memory. Allow God to speak into your heart through that verse as you draw.

Prayer Mandalas

Begin with a circle ('mandala' means 'container of sacred essence').

Fill in the circle with your own patterns and art. You can also find mandalas with a template already drawn and all you need to do is color it in.

As you color, spend time in prayer. Ask God to be present and speak into your heart.

Don't worry about what you are creating. This is about the process of praying and spending time with God, not the end result.

Relax into the prayer. Allow your mind to wander through the thoughts God places on your heart.

Prayer Ideas...

For a more free-form way to pray through art, try praying through mandalas. This is an ancient form of prayer used across many religions. Praying through art allows you to express your prayers in different ways and helps the mind focus on God.

1) Draw your own prayer mandala. Start with a blank sheet of paper and draw a circle on it. Then, grab different colors as you feel led and begin to draw within the circle. Allowing your mind to focus on God and your prayers.

2) Color in a mandala template. You can find these online or in coloring books. As you color, let your mind clear and focus on listening to God. Lift your prayers to God as you color.

3) Journal about your prayer art. When you finish your art, journal about the picture. What does it mean in your life and how God is speaking to you through it? Pray about that and your response to God.

Prayer Ideas...

Select a favorite hymn or contemporary worship song. Choose one of the methods below to pray through the song.

1) Look up the lyrics and read through the words as a prayer. Try not to sing the song as you read, so you can pay attention to the words and what they mean to your life today.

2) Write out the verses that speak most profoundly to you. Pray through those words. Write them in your own words as your prayer.

3) Sing along with the song as your prayer, paying particular attention to the words. Sing the words as a prayer to God, considering how they relate to your own needs and responses to God.

4) Look up the scripture referenced in the song. (wordtoworship.com is a great resource). Pray through those scriptures.

Praying A Song

Hymns and worship songs are prayers to God. Many use words and imagery from scripture and can be a wonderful way to expand your prayer language.

Songs can be used in a number of ways in our prayers.

1) Sing your prayers as you sing the song. Listen to the words and sing them to God.

2) Read or speak the words, really thinking about what those lyrics say about God and about you.

3) Use the lyrics and scripture references to expand your prayer language as you pray through other methods.

Prayer Ideas...

The Taize Community is an ecumenical monastic order in France, with members from around the world. Taize-style prayer can be a beautiful and powerful way to spend time with God and meditate on His Word. Below are a few ways you can experience Taize prayer for yourself.

1) Attend a Taize service. Many churches offer Taize prayer services. Look around your area (even if it's not your denomination) and visit a Taize prayer service in person.

2) Listen online to the Saturday evening broadcast from Taize at www.taize.fr. Follow along with their prayer service.

3) Design your own Taize prayer time. Use the Taize songs or Gregorian chants as the music in your prayer time (available for purchase or find ones on YouTube). Or use familiar songs from your worship service at church.

Taize Prayer

Below is the typical structure of a Taize-style prayer time. The key characteristic of Taize music is the repetition of the words, making the music meditative and memorable. The singing becomes prayer.

1) Start with a song that is chant-like and meditative.
2) Read a passage of scripture.
3) Sing a song.
4) Time of silence to listen for God.
   This is the heart of the prayer service, so don't rush it. Reflect on the scripture. Allow God a space to enter your heart.
5) Sing a song.
6) Pray intercessory prayers.
7) Close with the Lord's Prayer.

Find more information at www.taize.fr

Prayer Through Movement

Prayer isn't a passive activity. It's not something you just do quietly and then move on with your life. Prayer changes lives - yours and others. Prayer calls you to make changes and take steps in your walk of faith. Prayer may ask you to step beyond your comfort zone and take action. Praying through movement becomes a metaphor for the action of prayer.

Prayer Through Movement Reflects Your Spiritual Journey

Prayer through walking is a powerful symbol of the spiritual journey. Your walk may have twists and turns, ups and down, stumbling blocks and detours. As you walk in prayer, such as through a labyrinth, you are reminded of that journey. While you may wander, God is directing your path. He will lead you back to Him. He will use every turn, detour, stumble, and pause for His purpose in your life.

Prayer Walking Moves You Closer To Those In Need

Prayer walking is a way to physically move you closer to those in need of your prayers. You can prayer walk through a neighborhood, through the pews of your church, through your school or workplace, even through the news headlines. It moves you from the comfort of your life into God's world.

Movement Awakens Your Senses and Brings Prayer To Life

Movement in prayer can take various forms. You can walk while you pray (even pray while running or exercising). You can explore different positions for prayer, such as sitting, kneeling, laying prostrate on the ground, or standing with arms raised to heaven. You can even use body motions while praying to correspond to your prayers.

These serve as more than movement, but as a way to physically connect with your spiritual senses. Your body positions can reflect the state of your heart. The movement in prayer awakens your senses on a different level to more fully connect with your prayers.

"True prayer is neither a mere mental exercise nor a vocal performance. It is far deeper than that - it is spiritual transaction with the Creator of Heaven and Earth."
~ Charles Spurgeon

Prayer Walk

Prayer walking is a form of intercessory prayer, praying for the world around you - in your city, in your neighborhood, in the news.

For a physical prayer walk:

- Walk with others, especially if you're in an unfamiliar neighborhood.
- As you walk, pray for those you pass by. Pray for each house, each person, each business.
- Pray for specific needs or simply for God's truth and blessings.
- Prayer walking should be low-profile. You don't need to carry a Bible or pray out loud. Just pray quietly as you walk.

Also try virtually prayer walking through the news, your email inbox, your social media feed, etc.

Prayer Ideas...

Below are ideas for prayer walking (both physical and virtual):

1) Walk through your neighborhood, praying over each family.

2) Walk around your school, praying specifically for each student and staff member. Bring a directory and pray for each by name.

3) As a group, prayer walk through an area of town in need of prayer.

4) Virtually prayer walk through the news, praying over each headline.

5) Virtually prayer walk through your Facebook or Twitter feed or email inbox, praying over each name you see and need you read.

6) Pray as you walk through your workplace, praying over each co-worker you pass by.

"Christ has no body now, but yours. No hands, no feet on earth, but yours. Yours are the eyes through which he looks with compassion on this world."
~St. Teresa of Avila

Prayer Ideas...

The labyrinth is an ancient spiritual tool for prayer and meditation. It can be a physical metaphor for your own spiritual journey, a pilgrimage 'in place'. It's not about getting to the center, but about walking with God.

1) **Find a physical labyrinth near you to walk.** Look in your community for churches or community spaces with a labyrinth. labyrinthlocator. com maintains a directory.

2) **If it's not possible to visit a physical labyrinth, print out a tabletop version and do a virtual walk with your fingers.** You can also find handheld versions to use in your prayer time.

3) **Decide how you want to experience the labyrinth and then enter in.** Use one of the options below to guide your experience. Let go of expectations and focus on the journey.

"Solvitur amvulando... It is solved by walking"
~Saint Augustine

Labyrinth

There is no right way to experience a labyrinth. You only need to enter and follow the path. Walk to the center, pause there and spend time with God, then follow the path back out. Below are a few approaches:

The "Inner Way"
- On the way in, pray for release - *"let go and let God"*
- At the center, pray for illumination - *"breathe on me breath of God, fill me with life anew"*
- On the way out, pray for the Spirit's guidance - *"Thy will be done"*

Ask a Question: Spend your walk praying and talking with God about a particular question or concern weighing heavily on your heart.

Gracious Attention: Quiet your mind and walk, letting go of all thoughts. Listen for God's voice as you walk.

My Favorite Methods and Places for Prayer

Use this page to take noes on your favorite methods and placed for prayer for different occasions. Use this list for inspiration and ideas on days you're not sure what to pray.

For Every Day Prayer:

_____
_____
_____
_____
_____
_____
_____
_____
_____
_____
_____
_____
_____

To Listen For God's Response:

_____
_____
_____
_____
_____
_____
_____
_____
_____
_____
_____
_____
_____

To Worship & Praise God:

_____
_____
_____
_____
_____
_____
_____
_____
_____
_____
_____
_____
_____

To Change Things Up:

_____
_____
_____
_____
_____
_____
_____
_____
_____
_____
_____
_____
_____

Kathryn Shirey

Kathryn Shirey is an ordinary girl following an extraordinary God, writing about prayer, trusting God, growing faith, and stepping into all of God's possibilities for your life at PrayerandPossibilities.com.

A recovering prayer skeptic who's experienced first-hand the power of prayer, she's passionate about guiding others to discover the transformation possible through prayer.

Find other devotionals and prayer resources at:
shop.PrayerandPossibilities.com

Connect with Kathryn:

Blog: www.PrayerandPossibilities.com

Facebook: www.facebook.com/PrayerandPossibilities

Pinterest: www.pinterest.com/kpshirey

Twitter: www.twitter.com/KathrynPShirey

Instagram: www.instagram.com/prayer.and.possibilities/

WITH KATHRYN SHIREY

Made in the USA
Columbia, SC
16 November 2023